RITA AN

IRELAND IS CHANGING
MOTHER

BLOODAXE BOOKS

ISBN: 978 1 85224 905 2

First published 2011 by
Bloodaxe Books Ltd,
Highgreen,
Tarset,
Northumberland NE48 1RP.

www.bloodaxebooks.com
For further information about Bloodaxe titles
please visit our website or write to
the above address for a catalogue.

Supported by
**ARTS COUNCIL
ENGLAND**

Cover design: Neil Astley & Pamela Robertson-Pearce.

Printed in Great Britain by
Bell & Bain Limited, Glasgow, Scotland.

For our grandson Óisín

ACKNOWLEDGEMENTS

Some of these poems or versions of them have previously appeared in the following publications: *Best of Irish Poetry*, ed. Matthew Sweeney (Southword Editions, Munster Literature Centre, Cork, 2010), *The Clifden Anthology* (2009), *A Festschrift for Pearse Hutchinson* (2007), *A Fine Statement: An Irish Poets Anthology*, ed. John McDonagh (Poolbeg, 2008), *Fusion* (USA, 2010), *The Graphic Studio, Hurting God* (Salmon Poetry, 2010), *The International Journal of Leadership in Public Services*, vol. 6 (2010), *The Irish Times, Oxfam Calendar* (2007), *La Paume Ouverte: A Festschrift for Françoise Connolly*, ed. Theo Dorgan (Poetry Ireland/Eigse Eireann 2010), *The Manchester Review, Poetry Review, Ploughshares* (USA), *The Salmon Anthology: A Journey in Poetry, 1981-2007*, ed. Jessie Lendennie (2007), *Shine Anthology*, ed. Pat Boran (Dedalus Press, 2011), *The Shop, The Stinging Fly*, and *Text*. 'Lottie Kelly Hot' was commissioned by *Ropes* (UK) in 2007.

Many of these poems have been broadcast on radio (RTE Radio One, *The Joe Duffy Show, Playback*, Lyric FM, Tullamore Radio and *Sunday Miscellany*) and on RTE Television (*Nationwide*, ed. Orla Nix).

Some of these poems have been translated by Bernhard Robben and can be heard on www.lyrikline.org.

Special thanks to Mikey Gannon (the computer man), Jessie Lendennie (Salmon Poetry) and Máirín Ní Dhonnchadha.

CONTENTS

9   Ireland Is Changing Mother

11   Lottie Kelly Hot

12   Burden of Proof

14   The Perfect Lash

15   He Was No Lazarus

16   Guilty

17   His Brazen Hair

18   Spectre

19   The Darkness

23   No Pity for Polyneices

24   TD on Local Radio re Expenses

26   Malaga O Malaga

28   Houdini

29   The Builder's Mess

31   O Sole Mio

33   The Fates

34   Chinese Notebook

35   Gawkers

36   Dirty Dancer

37   Visiting My Father at Christmas

40   Nearly Falling

41   This Was No Ithaca

44   The Prophet

46   Ping

47   The Pledge

48   The Immortals

49   Fahrenheit

50   Edict

51   Borders

52   Whitethorn

53   The Púca

54   Where Have All Our Scullions Gone

58   Hasta Libido Baby

59   No One Mentioned the Roofer

60   He Knows No Artichokes

61   Ask the Concierge

63   Tongued and Grooved

64 Hangovers Never Touched Him
66 Sea Dog
68 The Brent Geese Chorus
72 Oileán Na nDeor

Ireland Is Changing Mother

Don't throw out the loaves
with the dishes mother.
It's not the double-takes so much
it's that they take you by the double.
And where have all the Nellys gone
and all the Missus Kellys gone?
You might have had
the cleanest step on your street
but so what mother,
Nowadays it's not the step
but the mile that matters.

Meanwhile the Bally Bane Taliban
are battling it out over that football.
They will bring the local yokels
to a deeper meaning of over the barring it.
And then some scarring will occur –
as in cracked skull for your troubles.
They don't just integrate, they *limp-pa-grate*,
your sons are shrinking mother.

Before this mother,
your sons were Gods of that powerful thing.
Gods of the apron string.
They could eat a horse and they often did,
with your help mother.
Even Tim who has a black belt in sleepwalking
and border lining couldn't torch a cigarette,
much less the wet haystack of desire,
even he can see, Ireland is changing mother.
Listen to black belt Tim mother.

When they breeze onto the pitch
like some Namibian Gods
the local girls wet themselves.
They say in a hurry, O-Ma-God, O-Ma-God!

9

Not good for your sons mother,
who claim to have invented everything
from the earwig to the *slíothar*.
They were used to seizing Cynthia's hips
looking into her eyes and saying
I'm Johnny come lately, love me.

Now the Namibian Gods and the Bally Bane Taliban
are bringing the local yokels
to their menacing senses,
and scoring more goals than Cú Chulainn.
Ireland is changing mother
tell yourself, tell your sons.

slíothar: hurling ball

Lottie Kelly Hot

I could see the way you were
when you were texting him
at the bus stop – sheepish way.

Your school bag thrown there
the way you threw me – forsaken way.
You leaning backwards using the bus shelter
the way you used me – slovenly way.

And when the bus came
you tossed your mane back
the way you tossed me – jerky way.
Your bulls-eye-striped-tie lolling
over your white shirt – succulent way.
Your pleated skirt shorter than a hiccup – wow ways.

Your luscious legs
Eiffel Tower bound – sky ways.
Your knee socks sliding down town – Lottie Kelly Hot way.
Lottie Kelly hot you take the biscuit – a lot ways.
You take me not a jot, not a little not a lot – misery ways.

Burden of Proof

You want a ticket please, with concessions.
What are you, unemployed or unemployable?
Can I see your unemployed card?
Sorry you seemed to have mislaid it.
Well I'm sorry too, I need proof,
just because you are standing there in front of me
dripping wet and sneezing
doesn't mean that you get concessions, ya prick.

Now go away and get proof
that you are human and unemployed
and come back and show me that proof
and then I will give you the ticket
for two euros cheaper
and wipe your nose, you snivelling git.

You genuinely forgot it,
and could we make an exception this time?

This is the Black Box
this is an Abbey Play
we don't make tea
we don't make devil's doughnuts
(unless it's in the script)
we don't make exceptions,
we make decisions
to uphold the concessions law.

Who'll pay Mark O'Rowe
for all that rape and rancour
if we let you in without proof.

My advice to you, ya prick:
go home and find proof,
that's if you have a home,
from where I stand
it looks like you could easily fit
inside an ear of corn.

Check your mongrel's mouth
check the cats Melaka
check your Daideo's bunghole
but get proof,
then come back and enjoy the show.

The Perfect Lash

She asked the man in the photo hut
to fix this photo of her mother.
You can't see her eyes,
I want to be able to see my mother's eyes
is it too much to ask?

Do you have another photo of her
with her eyes in it, he said?

I'm afraid not this is the only one I have.

A few days later
she came back for the photo.
She was pleased at first.
Soon she noticed
they weren't her mother's eyes.

Her mother as everyone knew
had a big heart,
but she had glaucoma and styes
now she has long lashes.
Sophia Loren's eyes.

He Was No Lazarus

(for Niall MacMonagle)

In the newsagents come bric-à-brac
days were spent gawking out
hoping the girls would come in for a chat
or any old gossip that would help throttle
a jaded afternoon.

I smoked nearly as many cigarettes as I sold
and what I didn't sell, I gave away.
The Shantalla gang came in ones and twos
'give us a fag loveen' and I'd give them twenty.

Once I gave Elvis Kelly a yo-yo
to pass the time until he went to England.
I'll give you one long snake kiss for it, he said.
They all went to England on the half three out of Galway.
We were like banshees crying over them
then we lived for the S.W.A.L.K. letters.

Harlesden got him and plenty more besides;
he drowned his sorrows in The Green Man.
A right yo-yo, he fell under his own weight and broke his skull.
A maverick blood vessel made the same noise as a cork
pop went his flash lights and he all fell down.

When he went down he stayed down, ton of bricks style,
he was no Lazarus, no shape-changing Greek or Roman God
no comic book super villain who could say,
Abra Kadabra now you see me now you don't.

He was no Zossima either, though he wore the brown
scapula of our lady of Mount Carmel around his neck.
He came home in a box, spartan no frills
just a shiny plate with his name, his date of birth.

I was one long snake kiss out of pocket.

Guilty

I was young
I was afraid of everything
the magazines were coming:

The Far East
The Irish Messenger of the Sacred Heart
and the rest of them.
I was four or five years old
the magazines were coming
everyone in the house was going to confession
going to mass
everyone was sad.
They said to God
we are sad God.
I was young
I was sad too
I said to God
I'm sad God.
Something was happening
the magazines were coming
bread and jam was plentiful in the house
the magazines were plentiful
I was afraid of everything
I was guilty
the hens were guilty
the dogs were guilty
the stones were guilty
the line in the middle of the road was guilty
the well was guilty
we drank from it
we were all guilty.

His Brazen Hair

I was looking at the Brian Bourke exhibition
in the Fairgreen Gallery.
Outside a man lay collapsed on the ground.
It was freaking people out
they kept coming in telling the person
at the desk about the man on the ground.

After a while the guards came,
they were wearing blue gloves.
They knew the body on the ground.
They poked him with the blue gloves.
Get up Gerry, get up outta that.

Don't you know
there's an exhibition on in there Gerry
and you are making a right exhibition
outta yourself out here.

Gerry didn't you know the Arts Festival was on
he didn't know about Brian Bourke's nudes.
Otherwise he might have washed his face
patted down his brazen hair
pulled himself together.

Spectre

I think of Peter Porter
in the Atlanta Hotel.
He said he had nightmares
all night.

Some shade
tried to steal his muse.
A local *taibhse*
who could walk through walls.
Ghouls and harpies came with him,
all second cousins.

I told him about this cold spot
in the hall of a convent
where a shiver flies past.

Double takes
yield nothing
neither does
listening harder.
There's barely a sound;
save the odd whirr
nearly a hum
as good as a hiss.

Go on, he says, his arms folded.

taibhse: ghost

The Darkness

It was early Christmases
it was perjury lights
it was let's organise the masses
it was death by devotion
it was googleability talk
it was doctor only cards
it was hailstones
it was gallstones
it was clamping
it was glamping
it was jackstones
it was January sales
it was complex stuffing
it was dishcloth dreams
it was back on the dole queues
it was Fás schemes
it was refuse charges
it was Fás expenses
it was soap operas
it was pope operas
it was Spiddal in the middle
it was rain rain rain
it was kidney stones
it was Neven Henaff
it was tribunals
it was lost receipts
it was a limo, here a limo there
it was SSIAs
it was Irish Nazis
it was grey days
it was boy racers
it was MRSA days
it was Namaphobia
it was mimicry Sunday
it was how are u texts
it was ex, it was pect
it was ations

it was swine flu
it was birdie flu
it was real male
it was single male
it was jingle mail
it was Biffo's budget
it was Robo cop direct / not
it was bailout or pale-out
it was paper profit
it was cranks, it was foreign-owned banks
it was inside information
it was an act of contrition
it was nasty it was undo-plasty
with your family who had affluenza.
We adore thee O Lend-A-Hand we bless thee
because by bailouts thou hast saved our deposits, not.
It was Lesbos, besbos, no to Lisbos.
it was Aer Lingus
it was Michael Cunny O'Leary.
it was broken teeth
it was singleton mail
it was Fingleton mail
broken storage heaters
a season for grieving
a season for thieving
it was cryptosporidium
it was Mama, it was Nama
it was all Hail Obama
it was cancer centres of excellence (my eye)
it was never the HSE
it was centres of chaos
it was lead in your water
lead in your tea
overcrowding in hospitals
it was never the HSE
it was sore heels
it was cold sores
it was credit crunch
it was balefuls, bailouts

it was stag nites
it was stag nation
it was stag flation
it was a new four letter word
starts with an F and ends with with a T
financially untouchable funt
you funting funt, or you dirty rotten funting funt
it was homophobia
it was nomophobia
it was home alonia, single male gingle mail
it was six banks full
we adore theee o cash we non-ebrities
it was high cholesterol
the weight of your sins
the weight of your bins
it was doomers, poofers, moofers,
it was out of work roofers
it was good bye Polish cleaners
we're back on the dolers.
It was momnesia
it was sly tox, boytox, my socks
it was 900 euro a night hotels in Venice
it was chauffeurs to Cheltenham
it was take me from terminal one to terminal three
but don't put me in with the plebs
it was take me to Kerry but put me in a plane
it was Dublin to Cannes
Cannes to Kerry
Kerry to Cardiff
Cardiff to Cannes
Cannes to Northolt
Northolt to Dublin
it was a conference on women in poverty in China
but make my hotel five star
it was I can and I will
and I'll do it again
it was more green tea, fat free
it was on your knee economy
it was never the HSE

the worst has yet to come
said George Grimm Reaper deeper Lee
it was never the Government
it was An Tuatha Nua, An Bua
An Bord Snip Nua.

No Pity for Polyneices

(for Irene Gilsenan Nordin)

In a small churchyard in Leksands,
the funeral cortège
slip away in their magpie vestments.
Leaving the coffin perched there.

They will be back for the ashes
in five maybe six days.
Same black and white clobber
same aura paura.
No pity for Polyneices.

In the very-mean-time
people the deceased didn't know
arrive dressed in more smartness 'n' tartness
they have no snakes in their hair
no Cyclops eye.

These are designer genus pica,
they clack with the souls and heels
they flick with the tongue
they click with molars to die for –
they side step each other
begging gardens and pardons.

I beg your smartness,
not at all I beg your tartness.
All in good mortal time
swanking in and out
clack clacking as they go.
Taking the flowers from coffin to kerb.

TD on Local Radio re Expenses

Thanks for agreeing to come
on the programme this morning.
I thought you'd be wrecked after the golf yesterday.
Anyway I have to ask this or the listeners will kill me,
why are your expenses so high?

But they are not really my expenses
they lump my secretaries wages onto that equation,
and that's a lot of secretary to have to lump in I have to say.

Now now, you're on the radio not on the golf course,
you're an awful man altogether
let's get back to your expenses, ha ha.

O there's my phone now,
you see, that's one of my constituents trying
to get through to me
they are always trying to get through to me
I'm getting counselling after all them constituents
ringing me all the time.

Not from a fellow councillor I hope, ha ha.
Now let's get back to your expenses.

Them constituents think they own ya
just cos they vote for ya.
I was down in the G Hotel
having one of those treatments done
the other day.

What kind of treatment?

It's there in my expenses
I was having my back, sack and crack done
and my phone rings and this one
is shouting down the phone at me

24

about how the sewer outside her door is
all clogged up and the smell has nearly killed
her Staffordshire pit-bull

But what about your expenses ?

I'd love to talk about my expenses
but I have a dental appointment.
My wife says I grind my teeth in my sleep
my dentist says all my teeth have jagged edges.
Did you see that film jagged edge,
it was brilliant, absolutely brilliant?

Your an awful man can we get back
to the issue of your expenses, ha ha?

It's not me that spending all that money
it's office equipment for my secretary
she likes to swing her legs over backwards
and catch a rugby ball between her teeth,
you know that machine what's it called?

The shredder is it?

No no no, it's called *power plate*
but she knows who has the real power here,
and less if your sarcasm
or I might well ask you who owns this station, ha ha?

I have nothing to shred
I have nothing to hide,
it's my secretary, her wages and all that
the equipment she uses so that one day
she can fit through the eye of an needle
the poor thing.

Malaga O Malaga

(for Marion Moynihan)

I am a goose on one leg
waiting at Malaga airport.
No one will notice that I'm a goose
because Malaga airport is full of geese
standing on one leg,
and it's always the left leg.

The noise at Malaga airport has a cadence
a loud loud lisp
and a cac-cac-cackle,
all thunder no rain.
Some noises are necessary
if we want to see the other birds,
and we all want to see the other birds.
We have to put up with the noise
aren't we making half the noise ourselves?
So many geese together
so many wild geese.

I stick my neck out
I have a neck like a swan
a shrink once told me.
My father used to say
I had a neck for anything but soap.
I stick my neck out to see
if the other bird has landed.
The rest do the same thing
they stick their necks out.

The odd cratur hops on the other foot
but we take no notice.
Hardly anyone hisses
except two old codgers
who fell fowl of the flock years ago.
They were leaning against the back wall
complaining about air miles
and the journey south
scratching their tail feathers.

You could forgive them that
this waiting is wearing on the nerves.
Loved ones are coming for Christmas
the expectations terrify
the noise is now more whooper than hubbub.
It blocks out everything
except what the eyes can see.
All the eyes are on the arrivals gate
and on the electronic noticeboard
landed, delayed, landed, delayed,
landed delayed landed
which is it, which is it
we all stretch our swans' necks.

It's hardly a sanctuary here
but all those open arms
harness their own remedy.
A veinless threadless remedy
that needs no water or air to flourish.
Just those outstretched arms,
and a dash of something
unseen unheard,
made from lonely
made from loss.

We were alone for nine hundred years
now all those loving collisions
are turning us into right ninnies.
We are sobbing and bobbing
and all over happy and secure
but our clothes are all creased.

The teenagers aren't goslings anymore.
But they are still whooping
and the noise is all thunder no rain
people are getting hugged
right left and centre, arms outstretched
loving collisions are happening
feathers are flying
all over Malaga airport.

Houdini

Today I was on the train
where no one could needle me.
My thoughts could run amok
or they could slide easily into Corcomroe Abbey.
I could climb Pollatomish from here
or crawl into my favourite soap.

Today I didn't need a place to park guilt.
I didn't need to disinfect over and over
my thoughts could stay filthy.
I could run out of things not to say.

Today I was on the train,
where oncology couldn't touch me.
After all it was only a word that went in deep
like a cannula, or a drip.

The Builder's Mess

Toxic and tired is the builder's mess
in post-Celtic-tiger-Ireland.
Now that the bubble's burst mother
the ghost-estates are everywhere.

A bank-owned-builders'-mess mother.

All those estates
six hundred and twenty, maybe more,
few finished, loads unfinished.
Unsightly and neglected
dirty-faced and dour mother
toxic and tired mother.

The Olympic rats run in and out
of unfinished drainpipes,
up bare-stairs,
devouring lagging jackets
in hot presses that never had heat.

Someone high up in a department,
reeking with negative equity
calls all the ghost estates,
a phenomenon mother.

The homeless guy who is barred
from the homeless shelter
for urinating in a doorway.
He calls them a shame mother
a crying shame mother.

Some were completed and vacant,
some were found to be occupied
some were found to be empty and occupied,
all at the same time mother.
Others were bought but never built mother.

And what do the sons and daughters
of the Celtic tiger call them mother?

The ones who camped out in the floods
to get the semi with the decking,
and the snooker table lawn mother.
The ones who queued
with their deposits in their pockets,
their unborn children up their sleeves
their shaved backsides hanging out.
What do they call them mother?
They call them a travesty mother.

O Sole Mio

My friend was having an affair
with a married man.
They used to do it
in an old warehouse at the docks,
before the Celtic Tiger got teeth.

As she undressed
he likes to sing Mario Lanza,
and afterwards
when she was having her fag
it was more Mario.
She always said, Bravo,
blowing smoke in his face.
They laughed.
Sometimes they did it twice
and for the big finish
he'd blast out Santa Lucia.

It ended badly
when his wife found out.
They say she gave him
a dig in the mouth at mass
knocking out his gold tooth.

Others say she took
a pinchers
to his precious parts,
squeezing so hard
it stymied his voicebox.

Years later I met her in Zhivago Records,
in the aisle between the tenors
and the five-for-twenty-five box sets.

I asked her how was he now.
She didn't know, only she heard
he was spotted a few times,
walking around the new docks
his hand in the air, his mouth open,
miming like mad.

The Fates

The fates are on a bank holiday weekend
showing off around the long wards.
The spinner spins herself
into a menacing match with a melanoma
(more like a blip really).
Sourface Atropos is dying her hair,
bile green with a streak of infection.

I wouldn't mind another look
at that lump on your husband's neck
I love lumps me, the doctor said.
The spinner is spinning like Michael Flatley,
her dress is all fatigue and scans
her look is pins and needles.
Could he come to my clinic on Tuesday?
He can go straight to the top of the queue
I just want another feel of that lump
I love lumps me.

The measurer measures her cloth
to suit her covered-in-bling balaclava.
It fits oddly over her radiation mask.
I might admit him
but it's nothing to worry about.
Sourface Atropos never turns over a new grief
never turns up her nose to a barium meal
never turns.

Chinese Notebook

Two stops to Maoist temple
three stops to Buddhist temple
four stops to Versace temple

the egret
and the heron
could care loads
could care less

the crested Bulbul
old man
too old for sex
too able for berries

Qi lou
fifteen strokes
for the seventh floor
not counting
the seven

Chinese pond heron
old man
with brittle bones

common kingfisher
out all night
today it perches

rice noodles and beer
an egret
walks on eggshells

the crested goshawk
any lizard
any rat

Qi lou: seventh floor

Gawkers

We glided through the green water
of Tai O village in a tunnel boat.
Some of us were lean
some of us were leaner.

We were falling over ourselves
with our slick new digital cameras.

The boat people played cards
in their houses on stilts –
some of them were quiet
some of them were quieter.

We took pictures
of the barnacles
and the people playing cards
in the houses on stilts.

Two egrets lamped us,
they flew south
their carriages straight
their beaks cocked.

Some of the card players
nearly looked up
Some of them didn't.

Dirty Dancer

In the Tai Chi garden
in Hong Kong
an old man –
the only smoker there
flicks through a porno magazine.
He has a huge wart on his lip.

His laidback, scratch my arse,
bite me look says to anyone
who wants to read it:

Better to be in the park with porn
than four-walling it on the 80th floor
the icicles of lonely
jerking at my heels.

Visiting My Father at Christmas

How hard could it be?
Duck in, a bit of small talk
duck out, dodging the bullets
and fire a few myself
how hard could it be?

The booby traps are under
the Quality Street box.
Tread softly, start again.
it will be easy
a piece of cake,
dyspepsia maybe
or no heart scald at all

A short journey
or a long haul,
the choice is mine.
Watch out for black ice
by nature sly
by day a looking glass.

There are no footpaths
no kerbs to fall off
this territory is wide open
a plate under foot.

Words matter;
words don't matter
speak when you're spoken too.
Spokes are a snare
silence is the hardest station.
Remember the fifth commandment.

Plenty to talk about
the frost, the treachery of ice
the black ice.

The heat of the room
the great fire,
that's a great fire
the Quality Street
and who brought them.
The new couch and chairs.
That's a lovely couch, is it new?
the great fire,
we did the fire already,
next get-out clause where are you?

The television,
same bloody programmes every year.
That television is going back.
The turkey, yeah the turkey
tough as the sole of my shoe
mind you the stuffing was champion
the ham, yeah the ham.
a pillar of salt.

Then the more mundane.
Do you know anything
that will get rid of heartburn?
Snakes and bladders.

Then down to the knitty bitty,
he was working up to it
lifting the head as if to say something
then saying nothing.
Silence is a tough station.

I had that heartburn
two years ago when you called as well.
Where did you get that cape outa?
Strange looking yoke for a girl to be wearing.
Is it second-hand?
People wear anything nowadays
any old rag at all,
it looks like a shroud.

It would look good on you then.

You were sharpening your tongue
for a week for that one, he'd say
I'll bet you don't know the Irish for shroud though!

The years between us
ticked and tocked, snaked and bladdered
down the whole gastric acid afternoon.
The Christmas tree glistening
the talking clock saying nothing,
not a hiccup at all.

Nearly Falling

In the TB ward
on Christmas Day
we settled down
for telly time.

Delia said over and over,
Charlie Charlie, chap chap chap.
How can he be on telly
when he's dead?

We kept watching the telly.
Delia kept up her rant.

One of the patients said,
shsssush Delia.
Then we all started.
Yeah Delia,
Shut the fuck up.

Don't you shuussssh me
you streals of misery
with sputum mugs to match,
I've seen better looking bodies
on half-eaten crows.

You're watching a dead man dancing
waddling on the soles of his feet,
nearly falling and not falling.
And you don't see anything wrong with that!

You sit there
'Mary Melancholies'
your jelly babies
your blankety blank eyes
your jam jaws.

This Was No Ithaca

The women of Baile Crua
never filled their heads
with yellow and pink rollers
letting on to be going somewhere
when their was no somewhere to go.

Somewhere was where other women went
women with magnolia vision
and pencil shaped dreams
and always a jezebel cigarette
between those blood-red lips.

The women of Baile Crua
filled their heads
with a loving Godling
whom they duly served
every waking second.

They implored their loving Godling
to follow their vagabond sons
down the alleyways of Cricklewood
and Camden Town and further afield.

If the pencil shapers
turned the heads of the husbands
and if the husbands called out the wrong name
when they were claiming their god given rights,
what harm was it for God's sake.

It was fine with the women
who never filled their heads
with yellow and pink rollers
and never let on to be going somewhere
when there was no somewhere to go.

These women were busy imploring
their loving Godling
to keep their daughters in a state of grace
until the wedding night
and not allow shame to fall on the family
by letting any daughter of theirs
waddling down the aisle
with a belly full of baby.

For the favours sought from
their loving Godling
the women with no rollers
would wear their knuckles inside out
making God's altar shine.

And God's marble was a sheet of ice
and the husbands whose heads were
pencil shaped turned
saw themselves in it when they went up
to receive the body of Christ.

The women of Baile Crua
made many sacrifices,
and the deity was always the same,
their own Godling.

He kept them on their toes
they praised him often
at door steps with arms folded
at bus stops and at the solemn novena
and any place that resembled a cross,
ditch, *bóithrín* or bog.

Except for Missus-all-over-Hurt
who had no deity that wasn't
in a small brown bottle
that brought instant rapture
when she tossed three or four
of them beauties onto her palm.

They took away the rasping pain
of the day the other women's God
let her only son kiss the face of a raging truck.

This was no Ithaca
no sweat was ever broken
trying to reach here.
You could get here by taking
a bus from Eyre Square
and collecting your parked bike
from a friend's garden
and cycle the last mile.

There was no Poseidon here
to blow a hole in your dreams
this was a place you didn't need
rollers in your hair for,
letting on to be going somewhere
where there was no somewhere to go.

This was Baile Crua
all you needed was a loving Godling
to polish and die for.

bóithrín: a boreen, a small road.

The Prophet

(i.m. Anne Kennedy)

I see things me.
I have to be observant in my job.
Taxi drivin' isn't just choking a gear stick
and knowing the racing results.

See this weather, I saw it comin'.
it was the bees that tipped me off
my wife says I'm clairvoyant.
I noticed every time I passed the hedge
in the girlfriend's house,
I could hear the bees buzzing like crazy.

The girlfriend says when you're in love
you hear all sorts.
The wife is more of a home alone drone,
but not without a sense of humour,
She says 'Are they buzzing for ya today pet?'
I still have sex with the wife
I give her the odd sting all right
I don't tell the girlfriend though
she'd go mental.
I tell her I sleep on the couch.

If she lamps the wife with that belly on her
that'll be the end of my fortune telling,
what she doesn't know won't bother her.

I wouldn't hurt a fly me.

Servicing the two of them has me worn out.
There are more bees around this year –
nasty weather comin' I'd say,
don't need a weathercock to forecast that.
I see things me, the wife would testify to that.

This place is a right Sodom and Gomorrah
the things that goes on in this town
would make a Buddha blush

One day the dog was trying to get a bee off his back
he was putting his paw back like this
it was gas to look at.
I watched for ages and ages.
I could have smacked the bee
with a rolled up newspaper there and then
and bet his brains out.
But if I missed my mark
the two of us would have got stung,
no point in that.

Ping

Missus Sugar Lump
never allowed dust to visit,
and creepies did not crawl in her house.
The exception was one fake lucky bag beetle
she left on the mantelpiece
to make herself laugh on wet days.
She was the future.
She had an abundance of hair nets
several shades of brown
no one could tell the difference
but she could, a shade darker is a shade darker.
She wore a corset
that helped her chin stay slightly skyward.

She had doilies
when we were just coping
with running water and flush toilets.
She was the future.
When she had the stations in her house
a pup from down the road
put his hand in the sugar bowl
and took out a fistful of cubes.

She said, watch this, to Missus-Box-Pleat-Curtains.
And with a silver teaspoon
she rasped hard on down-the-road's-knuckle.
You never need to beat them up
when they misbehave,
you just get that teaspoon
pretend it's a tuning fork,
and listen to it ping.

The Pledge

It didn't matter
who got the sisters the 'Baby Power'.
Any youngster who was passing
was sent up the hill to Hogan's pub.
A promise of two pence for themselves.

When one of the sisters died
the other two got into the bed beside her.
Well tanked up with their favourite tipple
they fell asleep.

That story did the rounds
about them going to bed with a corpse.
The sisters couldn't care less,
they didn't fear the dead,
they feared the man with the book
who called every week.

He touched the pencil on his tongue,
a sentence with fractions.
They peered at the small print,
the story of their lives.

The Immortals

The boy racers
quicken on the Spiddal road
in Barbie Pink souped-ups
or roulette red Honda Civics.
With few fault lines or face lifts to rev up about
only an unwritten come hither of thrills
with screeching propositions and no full stops –
if you are willing to ride the ride.

Hop you in filly in my passion wagon.
Loud music and cigarette butts are shafted into space.
We'll speed hump it all the way baby
look at me, look at me
I'm young, I'm immortal, I'm free.

Gemmas and Emmas,
stick insects or supermodels,
regulars at 'Be a Diva'
for the perfect nails,
eyebrows to slice bread with,
and landing strips to match.

They wear short lives
they dream of never slowing downpours
while half syllable after half syllable
jerk from their peak capped idols lips.
Their skinny lovers melt into seats
made for bigger men.
Look at me, look at me
I'm young, I'm immortal, I'm free.
The boy racers never grow older or fatter.

On headstones made from Italian marble
they become: 'Our loving son Keith'
'Our beloved son Jonathan,' etcetera etcetera.
On the Spiddal road
itching to pass out the light
they become Zeus, Eros, Vulcan, Somnus.

Fahrenheit

A cloud drapes itself over Tuar Beag,
nearly sending me under the table.

Last night the clocks went back an hour.
I say obvious things like
it will soon be dark at four
and other mundanes.
We can hardly walk the bog now.

I feel like Iris of the Lost Rainbow
spoiling for a storm.
I can hear you shouting at the horses on TV
you don't hear what I'm saying
but you reply anyway,
'yeah it was a rotten year for blackberries'.

When the summoned gusts
blow down the *bóithrín*
and rip the buttons off your shirt
you'll care then,
your wide-screen in the ditch

Aeolus comes without *plámás*
loyal wind bag that he is.
The squall gains strength
galvanise roofs, loose teeth
creaking jaw joints
ice-sheets and whirlwind,
a Connemara cyclone.

plámás: flattery

49

Edict

Go to Tuar Beag and sing for her.
Take only left turns
pass out the whitethorn
but remember to pay homage,
admire it as it should be admired
pay no heed to the piseog brigade.

Stay with her *lon dubh*, perch and be ready.
Watch out for straws in the wind
egg shells, a lone magpie
a wendy goat, mistletoe out of season.

Keep an eye on Regret
jaywalker by day, shape shifter by chance
and Despair, a weasel waiting to lunge.
Settle and sing blackbird, sleep not.

lon dubh: blackbird; *piseog:* superstition

Borders

There's no hope of a joy rider here
no one wears broken glass on their back walls
here there are no back walls
no front walls, no fences with menaces
no Rottweilers, no child-eating Dobermanns,
no pinch of tension in the air
that sets fire to a good night's sleep
no jumpiness that incites the joints
to early arthritis.

This is Pheasantville
easy peasy, *bóithrín* and bog
warbler boulevard
meander lane the pace the same.
The borders here are invisible
you'll find them rarely in the bend of a look,
the vexed angle of a grin
the crew-cut greeting,
the verb that takes longer to pall.

bóithrín: country lane

Whitethorn

Whitethorn is nearly covering Tuar Beag,
a christening blanket with thorns.
When I see it I think of my mother's warning.

'Don't ever bring whitethorn into the house
for fear it would bring the *mí-ádh* upon us
and attach itself to one of the youngsters
not yet walking but carrying their dividends of venial sin.'

(Do ye renounce Satan? We do)

The force, with no name or place in this dimension
might drag one of them angels down with the fever
or some fierce shaking calamity.

Unseen with the naked eye
the force could take one half of the twins
down to the fairy fort or further
into the fog in Coyne's field, never to be seen again.

'The lord protect us from all harm,
don't ever bring that whitethorn into the house.'

(Do ye renounce Satan? We do.)

Whitehorn: *mí-ádh:* bad luck
The Púca *(opposite):* *mar-dhea:* as if; *piseog:* superstition, a charm, or spell;
púca: a pooka, a sprite or ghost

The Púca

I asked my mother if it was a sign
of something that my communion veil
was sticking to Judy Connors' at the altar.

Herself and Mrs Burke with their arms folded
under their big cushioned breasts
were giving harem-scarum glances and *mar-Dhea* sighs.
They were at the start of laughing session
that would end with tears being wiped away
by the tail end of their flowery aprons.

And why wouldn't it be a sign
didn't my mother and her sisters in from Maree
talk in signs and piseogs all the time?
Every rickety move any Bally Brit bird made
was a sign of something or other.
Jackdaw, crow, magpie or maggot.

And if the goats shat on your dahlias,
God knows who was going to get an air mail letter
full to the brink with bad vowels and bile.
'God bless the mark' was used for everything, not just
when your neighbour's child had a strawberry birthmark
on their eyelid as big and bright as a peony rose.
And if anyone heard the Banshee's cry
that was it, some poor devil was a gonner.

Our days were one long piseog
and the Púca was there too to frighten the wits out of us.
It was the púca you would meet in all his malevolence
when you found yourself at the bottom of the well
if you dared poke your snout out after dark.

But good God, who never slept
was always flung like holy water
during a thunder storm, between you and all harm,
and the Púca like the cuckoo, could go and spit.

Where Have All Our Scullions Gone

It was hard hats and photo ops,
yella bellies and Gucci dreams
cutting ribbons on concrete schemes.
They were kissing babies
and talking roads,
they knew the bankers
would give them loads.

Why have one tunnel
when you could have two?
Or as any fool knows
two expensive tunnels
are better that none
bend over, spend over
let's have some fun.

Why have one motorway
when you could have four?
Not in your constituency
but in mine, that's fine.
Bend over, spend over
and don't fucking whine.

A motorway between
your dreams and mine,
another few motorways
just for the craic,
but never fix a pot-hole
on the back roads,
who'd be lookin at that?
Bend over, spend over
let's do it again.

This was the noughties
the boomers with beamers.
Decentralisation the edict –
go or be pushed.
Eleven thousand orders
but only three thousand went,
some in a cottage, some in a tent.

Millions for half empty offices
millions for fields
not a brick laid
not a thistle ever cleared.
Bend over, spend over,
let's do it again.

Let's buy Thornton Hall
for our gangsters galore.
At thirty million, it's a steal
not one dollar more.
The money was spent
not a brick was laid,
another twelve million
the legals were paid.

And why have one site
when you can have two?
Another twenty-six million
for a field near the zoo.
Bend over, spend over
it's time for a screw.

Get that pig out of the parlour
we need a place to bring guests.
Sheikhs and prime ministers
Presidents and Queens.
Farmleigh was bought
twenty million to start;
a kick in the liver
a punch in the heart.

Another twenty-eight million
just for dry rot.
Throw in asbestos
for a few million more.
Why stand on our feet
when you can nail us to the floor?
Bend over spend over
let's do it again.

One report first
then three reports more,
the legals were gushing
with jingle galore.
A watchtower went up
and it leaked from the start,
a dope ate the carrot
a dunce ate the cart,
One million, two millions,
twenty millions more.

A screen test for docklands,
what numpt ordered that?
The docu was scrapped
but the money was paid.
The *pleidhce* responsible
fiddled in the shade.

People's Mill Forest,
it didn't come cheap
pile up that dosh mountain
and make a big heap.
Glass bottle consortium
need a hundred mill more
in the honour of God.
Bend over spend over
let's do it again.

pleidhce: fool

A payroll system for the HSE.
They called it P. Pores
to make it sound smart.
despite all the millions
it never did start.

It was hard hats and photo ops,
yella bellies and Gucci dreams
cutting ribbons on concrete schemes.
They were kissing babies
and talking roads
they knew the bankers
would give them loads.

Hasta Libido Baby

I go to the supermarket
near Seedo's house,
to see if I could
get a glimpse
of his super body.

I'll wrangle my way
up the queue ahead of him.
He sees all the cat food –
he knows I don't have a cat.

I'd say, after you left
I went on the cat food.
It's delish, sometimes with sugar
sometimes with salt.

I do cold turkey
I do rabbit chunks.
It's great for the libido–Seedo –
he's bound to laugh.

No One Mentioned the Roofer

(for Pat Mackey)

We met the Minister,
we gave him buns, we admired his suit.
The band played, we all clapped.

No one mentioned the roofer;
whose overtime was cut
whose under time was cut
whose fringe was cut
whose shoelaces were cut
whose job was lost.

We searched for his job
but it had disappeared.
One of us should have said.

Hey Minister, we like your suit
have a bun, where are our jobs?
But there was no point,
he was here on a bun eating session
not a job finding session.

His hands were tied.
His tongue a marshmallow.

He Knows No Artichokes

She didn't mind his toxic tan
or his weasel taste in toothpaste.
What she did mind was
the way he'd Cheshire cat
the woman from the council,
and the way vice versa
would Cheshire cat him.

It was on the tip of her tongue
to tell vice versa,
that he was poison on the inside
and not to be fooled by his silk sheet face,
or them hammer your knickers to the ground eyes.

And furthermore when he tells you
he likes the Jerusalem artichokes,
forget it, the liary yoke knows no artichokes.
She has a good mind to tell vice versa
about his guacamole hole,
only she'd probably pity him.
He had a way of making the females pity him
a toxic tan way of touching the pity spot.

If they really knew,
his favourite food was
dried pigs blood with a thistle on top
and if he's not having a collision with a fry up
he's traumatised.

Jerusalem artichokes my crack.
Don't be fooled
by his silk sheet face, she'd say
he's rotting from the inside out
I know it and the street knows it,
the council should know it too.

Ask the Concierge

The demented walk tricky step here
jittery footfall, fractious jibe.
They bicker in the 'Everything for a Dollar Shop'.
Later when the energy is spent
they sit with their own selves
their underweight psyche.

One begs outside a shop called 'seduction'
underwear to raise the titanic.
Healthy looking mannequins with brazen breasts
balefuls of Canadian promise.
They come hither you
but you never come hither them.
Their chilling look deceptive,
their cherry lips,
kiss me, kiss me,
but only in your dreams loser.

Further down the street of the black squirrel,
a shop owner boasts about the underground.
You should see our underground
safest in the world,
no one ever gets plugged here.
In a doorway above Hades,
a policeman tells a man with no legs.
My name is zero tolerance
have you a licence for that rig?
My name is zero tolerance,
where is your mud guard?

The concierge have the real power here;
they take one look at your baggage,
one look at you, haversacks disgust them,
owners and trainers of haversacks
disgust them more.
Cross them and you will never see
one drop of Niagara fall.

They wide step and side eye you,
in their loose suits, hair oil up their sleeves,
their feet are made of sponge.
They deal in looks and eyebrow raising.
The Concierge code,
uncrackable to the luggage losers.

Back down on the high street,
I ask the man outside 'seduction'
if I can take his picture.
Don't ask me,
I have no picture to give or take,
what you see is what you get,
you see nothing you get less.

What the concierge seeks he finds,
he pirottes, he plucks, he spins he flies
where the concierge lives, the beggar dies.

Tongued and Grooved
(for C)

The look
was longing
was lustful
was lasting.

The kiss
was luscious
was lazy
was luptuous.

She staggered away
was woozy
was wanton
was wet.

Hangovers Never Touched Him

My father knew I had notions
long before I did.
I didn't like him much
but I liked him best
when he gave me a lift to work in town.

It was early morning, it was early May.
He was three sheets to the wind the night before.
There were four badgers in our scullery
and he was the four of them.

He embraced misery and doted on it like a pet lamb,
but hangovers never touched him.
This day he was quiet in himself
he was nearly kind.

This stillness he owned
paid for with years of yearning
waiting for the prodigal father to return.
The prodigal came and went
the stillness stayed, stoical and proud
like language, like land.

Not a word passed between us
all the bumper to bumper way
down Monivea Road
down passed the Greyhound Track
down passed St Patrick's Church
down passed the Magdalene Laundry
down passed Fox's Pub.

His stillness had a Sunday aura
the litany of saints.
A frugal sense
small talk was a weasel
big talk was a waste.

The forgiveness of sins
an illusion of knowing,
to thee do we cry poor banished children of Eve.

As I got out near the Skeff,
he said with mischief, but with no malice,
'Mind yourself Marlyn, mind yourself girl.'

Sea Dog

Novena traffic, damn
visiting time will be over.
Behind the River Inn,
the clampers wear
a grim-reaper-swagger.
Their faces lean with menace
a crooked-Galway-mile,

What to do! Will I park
or will I try somewhere else?
I'll have to chance it
I won't look back.

Somnus has sprinkled the ward again,
all eyes are closed.
Fatigue is a lovely dream.
I watch you sleep.
I wonder who you are
wearing a pirate bandana
and a purple drip.

I think of St Lucia and Heather's wedding.
The day we went on the pirate ship
the one used in *Pirates of the Caribbean.*
You topping up my watery wine
the steel band killing Bob Marley.

We saluted Helios
with our peaked capped hands.
We took his chariot on the high seas
and laughed at any old thing
all afternoon long.

Back now at the River Inn
I see the clampers
hi-ho-ing it in my direction.

I have no time to think,
only mortal rage.
The accelerator my broom,
I nearly mow them down.
I don't look back.

The Brent Geese Chorus

On the seventh day God rested,
and North Mayo was fashioned
and it had no likeness anywhere in the world.
And on the eight day along came Shell
at first with wheels and then with wings
and later with dozers, a lot of dozers
two-legged and four-legged.

They took long strides across your fields
measuring profit with every step.
Then they flew over, looking down, coveting.
A voice in wellingtons and a suit said,
People of North Mayo you will be rich
you will have jobs a plenty
the gravy train is coming
but we want your fields to park it in.

Those who didn't hear about it then
read about it later in the parish newsletter,
Gravy train heading at breakneck speed
first stop Erris. Last stop Clover Hill prison.
At first Shell worked through
the priest and the Bishop,
like the Holy Spirit.
The gas is coming
alleluia alleluia.

And it won't be ordinary gas
this will be great gas
raw and riveting,
it will trawl through your lives and your land
like a plague. It will wreck families.
Wives will feel the stress,
brothers and sisters will too
husbands will go to jail, for ninety and four days.

Why Erris! you asked *in ainm Dé*?
When we looked down on you, which was often,
we decided that you were the chosen ones
We saw a few geese, a whale or two,
an old dolphin on his last legs
and all that unspoilt beauty
waiting to be spoiled,
and god knows we can spoil.

And the letters started coming
loving letters, mister and missus letters
and everyone in Rossport was getting letters.
How is your cat and your dog and your budgie?
Our name is Shell and we care (*mar dheá*)
our name is Shell and we want what you have.

After a while loving letters changed from
we would like, to, we will have.
and what you don't give
we will take, and what's yours is ours.
and to hell with your budgie.

Wellingtons in the suit told you
he talked to you neighbours
and your neighbour signed.
Sign here on the dotted line
and don't look foolish on the ninth day
when all Erris will have signed but you.

The suits were grinning and saluting
waving and hooting,
and chanting at the crossroads.
God is good but gas is greater
sign here and be happy
na bac leis an dirty dolphin
what did he ever do for you?
Sign here like your neighbours over there.
sign here and have great gas.
God is good but gas is better.

We'll dig a few trial holes in your field.
They took first, and asked second,
We're from Shell on earth
we'll make life hell on earth for you and yours.
if you don't sign.
And there was a chorus of Brent Geese
singing all over Erris
Shell to hell, to hell with Shell,
and that chorus ran in and out of the bog
and it was everywhere in North Mayo.

We'll have insult-ations meetings
with you and your neighbours.
You can all come at different times
a divided people is better to us than a united people.
Come on your own so we can insult you on your own.
come together and we can insult you together.

As for your fields
let us in and let us at them
we'll even seed them for you.
They will be in better shape when we finish
than when we started.
A little hole here and a bigger hole there.
Pipe down here and away we go
or pipe down here and away we won't go.

Obscene words melted into Pollatomish
and other words sprouted.
Words like refinery, pipelinery, raw gas
terminal, three stage payment,
enterprise, outerprise, no prize, jobs my eye words.
No risk, no danger, no landslides
we can walk on stilts if we choose words.
And the government concurred.
God is good but gas is better
and if you don't sign we'll take you to court.
and the Brent Geese chorus started again.

And the Rossport families worried,
about the land and lake, the community,
Broadhaven bay, the Brent Geese and the whale,
the dolphin and the seal.

And the wellies in the clouds spoke again.
Our worthless word we give you freely
you won't even see the pipes going through your land
and the geese will live three hundred years.
We have great power we can walk on stilts.

Erris was angry, the deception was clear.
a ring of support was growing there,
they flung it far, they spun it wide
the Brent geese chorus never lied.
And Shell on earth made hell on earth
for the people living there
and some in the community considered flight
until the Rossport Five got up to fight.
The Brent Geese chorus never died,
the ninth day promised never arrived.

Shell on stilts with a swagger they stalk
onto your land without permission they go.
Can they drill on water,
is what Erris wants to know.

in ainm Dé: in the name of God; *mar dheá:* as if; *na bac leis:* never mind.

Oileán Na nDeor

For years he pinched sleep,
ate like a swallow,
he cried openly.

His memory was
that they took the Currach
on a day when the sea was all spite.
He tried to recall
what sparked the row.
Was it a comment he made about a girl
from a neighbouring Island
who loved them both?

He was the only
mortal left on the Island.
He watched like Argos night and day.

Lore has it,
he implored the vengeful sea
to give back his sons for burial.

Legend has it,
that on the night he died,
the half door was left open
the light was left on.

Oileán Na nDeor: Island of Tears